REVISED AND UPDATED

Plants & Fungi

Multicelled Life

Robert Snedden

Heinemann Library

Chicago, Illinois

Customer Service   888–454–2279

Visit our website at www.heinemannraintree.com

Designed by Kimberly R. Miracle and Betsy Wernert
Illustrations by Wooden Ark
Printed and bound in China by Leo Paper Group

12 11 10 09 08
10 9 8 7 6 5 4 3 2 1

New edition ISBNs: 978-1-4329-0033-5 (hardcover)
                     978-1-4329-0040-3 (paperback)

**The Library of Congress has cataloged the first edition
as follows:**
Snedden, Robert.
   Plants & fungi: multicelled life/ Robert Snedden.
      v. cm. -- (Cells and life)
Includes index
Contents: Different cells for different jobs: plant cells
-- The plant body: simple tissues, complex tissues, the
epidermis -- Stems: woody stems -- Looking at leaves: food
factories, photosynthesis, leaf specializations -- Roots -- A
new generation: sexual reproduction, flowers, pollination
and fertilization, seeds and germination -- Fungi: working
together.
   ISBN 1-58810-675-6 (HC) -- ISBN 1-58810-937-2 (Pbk.)
   1. Botany--Anatomy--Juvenile literature. [1. Botany--
Anatomy] 2. Plants--Juvenile literature. [2. Plants]
   3. Fungi--Anatomy--Juvenile literature. [3. Fungi] I. Title II.
Series.
   QK671 .S84 2002
   580--dc21

                                    2001008693

Acknowledgements
The publishers would like to thank the following for permission
to reproduce photographs: Garden & Wildlife Matters p. **21**;
Oxford Scientific Films pp. **5**, **8**, **13**, **14**, **16**, **19**, **24**, **25**, **27**;
Photodisc pp. **17**, **23**, **31**, **34**, **38**; Photo Researchers, Inc
p. **4** (David Nanuk); Science Photo Library pp. **15**, **22**, **33**
(J. Burgess), **37** (K. Kent), **39** (D. Scharf), **41** (A. and H-F.
Michler) **42** (S. Fraser), **7**, **10**, **11**, **20**, **32**, **43**; Stone p. **28**.

Cover photograph of a scanning electron micrograph
showing the pisil of a geranium wildflower, reproduced
with permission of MicroScan/phototake.

Our thanks to Richard Fosbery for his comments in the
preparation of this book, and also to Alexandra Clayton.

Every effort has been made to contact copyright holders
of any material reproduced in this book.
Any omissions will be rectified in subsequent printings if
notice is given to the Publisher.

Contents

Some words are shown in bold, **like this**. You can find
the definitions for these words in the glossary.

Different Cells for Different Jobs

A cell is a remarkable thing. A single cell alone is too small to be seen without the help of a microscope, and yet this tiny chemical package has all the properties of life. The plants and animals we see around us, and ourselves as well, are built from large groups of cells, millions and millions of them working together. Whether it be an oak tree or a daisy, a killer whale or a human child, all living things are made of cells. Cells are the units of life. They are life's building blocks. In this book we will be looking at how cells join together in plants and fungi.

Cell types

With optical microscopes, it is not possible to look in detail at the structure of a cell, but when powerful electron microscopes became available to biologists in the 1960s, they revealed some of the cell's most important secrets.

There are basically two types of cells. The simplest cells are the **prokaryotes**—the bacteria and **archaea**. These fast-working, living chemical factories have a simple structure—a thin outer membrane, and usually a strong cell wall, around a complex mix of water and chemicals.

The plant kingdom includes the Earth's oldest and biggest living things. Giant Sequoias (*Sequoia dendron giganteum*) are the biggest: a trunk can be 40 feet (12 meters) wide. They can also live for 3,000 years, although bristlecone pines (*Pinus aristata*) live even longer.

All other cells, including the other single-celled organisms and the cells that make up plants and animals, are more complex. The inside of the cells are divided into various compartments, called **organelles**. Each organelle carries out a variety of specialized tasks inside the cell. These more complex cells have another characteristic feature—the **nucleus**. This is a compartment containing the cell's genetic material, the information center that guides the cell's activity. (A few cells, such as phloem cells in plants and red blood cells, lose their nucleus when they mature.)

Cells with nuclei are called **eukaryotes**, a word that means "true nucleus." The prokaryotes (the word means "before the nucleus") are so-called because they lack a nucleus, along with other cell structures.

Becoming multi-cellular

It is possible that, many millions of years ago, the first multi-cellular organisms appeared when some single-celled organisms grouped together and formed a colony. To begin with, all cells in the colony would have been the same. But gradually different groups of cells would have taken on different jobs. This was the beginning of multi-cellular life.

In multi-celled plants and animals today, the billions of cells work together to support life. Some supply food, some transport food and wastes, others support the structure, and others have the job of producing the next generation. Cells of the same type form **tissues**. Several different tissues are combined in an organ, such as an animal's heart or brain. Groups of organs make up systems, such as the nervous system in animals or the **vascular** (transport) **system** in plants.

Being multi-cellular requires co-operation on a large scale. We see this co-operation working flawlessly all around us.

Plant Cells

A typical plant cell and a typical animal cell are similar in many ways. Both of them are held together by an outer skin. The skin of the cell is a thin **cell membrane**. In addition to holding the cell together, the membrane controls what passes in and out of the cell. It lets in some substances, but not others. For this reason it is described as a partially permeable membrane.

Animal cells come in a wide variety of shapes, but plant cells are usually boxlike or many-sided structures. This is because each plant cell is enclosed in a rigid cell wall. This is made of cellulose, a tough material that gives plants their strength. Where the plant cell surface is exposed to the air, waxes and other substances are produced to waterproof the cell. Inside the plant the cell walls are sticky and glue the cells together.

Both plant and animal cells have a large **nucleus**. This is the cell's control center. It guides the activities of the cell by providing instructions for building **proteins**. Proteins control the day-to-day activities of cells. A cell is essentially a tiny chemical factory, with hundreds of different chemical reactions going on at any given moment. Special proteins called **enzymes** control this chemical activity by altering the rates of the various chemical reactions that take place within the cell. Without enzymes, the reactions would virtually grind to a halt and life would cease.

Between the nucleus and the cell membrane is the **cytoplasm**. This is where the cell obtains energy from its food, carries out repairs, and makes new cell parts. The chemical reactions are constantly guided by instructions from the nucleus. Together, these reactions make up the cell's **metabolism**.

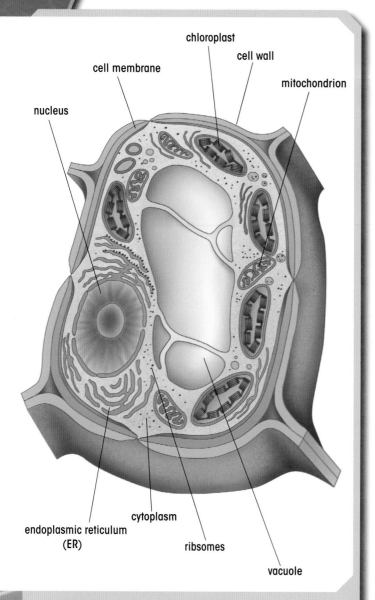

chloroplast

cell wall

cell membrane

mitochondrion

nucleus

endoplasmic reticulum (ER)

cytoplasm

ribsomes

vacuole

This diagram shows the features of a plant cell. The main features of a plant cell that are not found in animals are the cell wall, plastids such as chloroplasts, and the vacuole.

Plastids

In the cytoplasm of a plant cell there are some structures not found in animal cells. These are called plastids and there are three types: **chloroplasts**, **chromoplasts**, and **amyloplasts**. The chloroplasts are what give a plant its green color. They are full of light-trapping pigments called **chlorophylls**. Inside the chloroplasts the energy of sunlight is converted into chemical energy that is used to build sugars and other organic compounds.

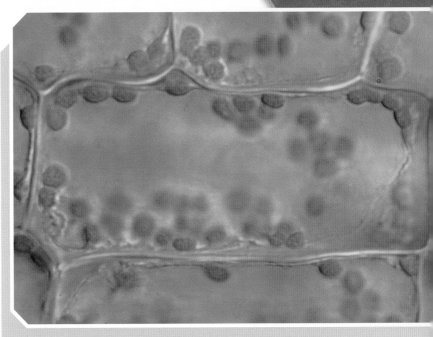

A micrograph of Canadian pondweed cells (*Elodea* species). The oval green particles within the cells are chloroplasts. Magnification approx. x 2,500.

Chromoplasts contain pigments of other colors. They give color to plant parts such as flower **petals**, ripening fruits, and fall leaves.

Amyloplasts do not have pigments. They are where some plant cells store food reserves in the form of starch grains. Seeds, as well as tubers and root vegetables such as potatoes and carrots, have an abundance of amyloplasts.

Central vacuole

Another distinctive characteristic of a mature plant cell is the **vacuole**. This is a large central cavity, filled with a watery fluid called cell sap and surrounded by a membrane similar to the cell membrane. The vacuole stores substances such as amino acids and sugars: chemicals that are vital for the cell's well being. The vacuole is also used to store toxic wastes that would be harmful to the cell if they stayed in the cytoplasm.

The central vacuole can take up anywhere from 50 to 90 percent of the interior of the cell. It pushes the cytoplasm up against the inside of the cell wall. This makes the cell turgid (firm and plump). When a plant has sufficient water all its cells are turgid, and this keeps the plant upright. If fluid is lost from the vacuole the cell collapses. We see this when a plant wilts because it needs water.

The Plant Body

Plants are a large and diverse group of organisms, but they all have a common characteristic that separates them from animals. Plants can make their own food from very simple ingredients in the soil and air. They do this by capturing energy from sunlight and using it to build the complex organic **molecules** that are a part of all living things. This process is known as **photosynthesis**. Because it can photosynthesize, a plant has no need to move around in search of food the way an animal does. All the energy it needs comes to it from the sun. This stationary lifestyle is reflected in the organization of a typical plant into two basic systems: shoots and roots.

A flowering plant

Almost all plants are flowering plants (the **angiosperms**). So, by and large, the structures discussed in this book will be those of flowering plants.

A flowering plant can be divided into two parts: the **shoot system** above ground and the **root system** below ground.

The shoot system can be further divided into leaves, stems, flowers, fruits, and other structures. Photosynthesis takes place in a plant's leaves. They are supported by the stem, which is also the main pipeline for water and **minerals** coming from the roots to other parts of the plant. Flowers are the plant's reproductive organs. Fruits develop from flowers, and are responsible for spreading a plant's seeds as widely as possible.

The root system spreads downward and outward through the soil. Roots absorb water from the soil, and also minerals—elements and simple molecules that are vital for making the large, complex molecules necessary for life. The roots also provide a firm anchorage for the shoot system above ground.

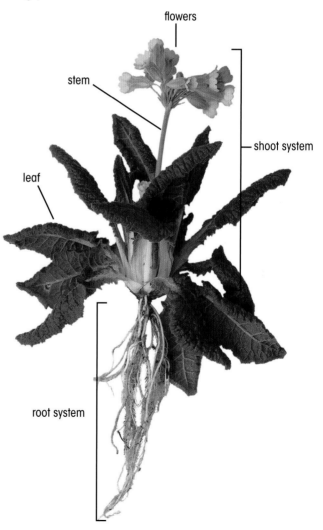

flowers

stem

shoot system

leaf

root system

The shoot and root system of a cowslip (*Primula veris*).

The plant kingdom

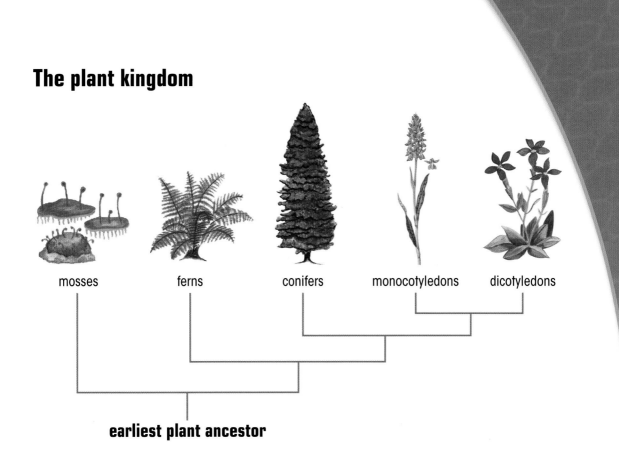

mosses   ferns   conifers   monocotyledons   dicotyledons

earliest plant ancestor

- The large majority of plants are flowering, seed-bearing plants (angiosperms). Roughly 360,000 of the 400,000 or so known plant species are classified as angiosperms. The angiosperms are divided into two major groups. The **dicotyledons**, or **dicots**, produce seeds that contain an embryo with two seed-leaves **(cotyledons)**. They have broad leaves with branched veins. Most herbaceous plants, such as lettuce and daisies, are dicots. Flowering shrubs and trees and cacti are also dicots. The **monocotyledons (monocots)** have seeds containing a single seed-leaf. They have narrow leaves with straight parallel veins. Orchids, lilies, palms, and grasses such as rice, wheat, and corn, are all monocots.

- The **gymnosperms** (naked seeds) are shrubs or trees: the most abundant of them are **conifers** such as pine, fir, spruce, and cedar trees. They differ from angiosperms because they have so-called naked seeds. This means they do not form a fruit around the seed, like flowering plants do. There are roughly 750 species of gymnosperms.

- **Bryophytes** are the second-largest plant group. They include plants such as mosses, liverworts, and hornworts. These are low-growing plants with leaf-like, stem-like, and root-like parts that lack the complex **tissues** found in flowering plants. There are roughly 19,000 species of bryophytes.

- Ferns, of which there are about 12,000 species, have roots and stems but do not flower. They produce spores on the undersides of their leaf-like fronds.

As in all multi-cellular organisms, large numbers of similar types of cells form **tissues** in plants. All of the parts of a flowering plant, whether stem, leaf, or root, are made up of three major tissue types.

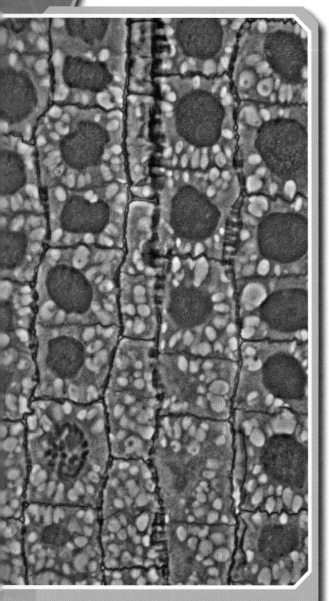

A light micrograph of the apical meristem of an onion root. The blue spots in the cells are **nuclei**. Some of the cells seem to have two nuclei: this is because they are in the process of dividing. Magnification approx. x 320.

- **Ground tissue** makes up the bulk of the plant. It is made up of mainly simple, unspecialized cells. The **photosynthetic** cells in leaves are ground tissue, as are the pith (innermost layer) of stems and roots, and the soft tissues in fruits.

- The **vascular tissue** system is the plant's plumbing, with the task of transporting water and dissolved substances to all parts of the plant. The veins in a leaf are made up of vascular tissue.

- The **dermal tissue** system is the plant's **epidermis** (skin) that covers and protects the outer surfaces of the plant. It can be as thin as a single layer of cells, or more than three feet thick like in the bark of giant redwood trees.

Meristems

Plant growth does not occur everywhere at the same time. Most of the growth in a plant occurs in special areas called **meristems**. Meristem cells are small and have few **vacuoles**. They can divide continuously.

There are two main types of meristematic tissue.

- meristems are found in the tips of roots, stems, and branches, and in flower and leaf buds. Growth from apical meristems increases the length of the root or shoot, and this is known as the plant's **primary growth**. Some of these cells will form other, more specialized cells.

- meristem tissue is found just beneath the outer layer of roots and stems, and is responsible for their thickening. This is known as **secondary growth**. One form of lateral meristem forms a sturdy covering that will replace the plant's epidermis.

Simple tissues

The ground tissue of a plant is made up of three simple plant tissues: **parenchyma**, **collenchyma**, and **sclerenchyma**. Each of these tissues consists of just one type of cell.

Parenchyma

The simplest plant cells are the nonspecialized cells called parenchyma. These cells are sometimes referred to as packing cells because they can fill spaces anywhere in the plant. Parenchyma cells are many-sided, and cube-like in shape. They have thin walls and are easily pushed out of shape by the pressure of cells around them. Tissue composed of parenchyma cells is referred to as parenchyma. Most of the primary growth of stems, leaves, flowers, fruits, and roots is made up of parenchyma cells.

More specialized cells in the plant lose their ability to divide as they mature, but parenchyma cells can divide throughout their lives. They are important for healing wounds in the plant. **Mesophyll** is a type of parenchyma that contains **chloroplasts** and is found in leaves. Other types of parenchyma are used for storage and as support tissues for the plant's **vascular system**.

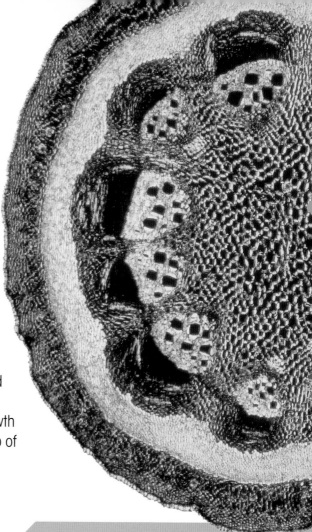

A light micrograph of a **dicot** plant stem in cross section showing parenchyma (yellow), collenchyma (gray outer ring), and sclerenchyma (grey inner ring) cells. Magnification approx. x 14.

Collenchyma and sclerenchyma

Collenchyma are elongated cells with unevenly thickened walls. Their role is to provide support. Collenchyma often form flexible ribs in leaf stalks, and provide an effective strengthening system for young plant tissues. The strands on the outside of a celery stalk are made up of collenchyma cells.

Sclerenchyma cells have extremely thick cell walls and provide rigid support for the plant. The thick walls of sclerenchyma are impregnated with a tough, waterproof material called **lignin**. Once the cell walls have thickened, the sclerenchyma cell dies.

Many seeds are also protected by sclerenchyma. The hard coating of a coconut shell and the pits of fruits such as cherries and peaches are formed by thick-walled sclerenchyma cells. Columns of long, thin sclerenchyma cells provide the structural strength to support stems and protect the cells inside from drying out.

Vascular Tissues

Complex **tissues** in a plant are those that are made up of more than one type of cell. Both the plant's **vascular system** (its transport network) and its **epidermis** (the skin), are classified as complex tissues.

The **vascular tissues** of a plant move water, dissolved **minerals**, and nutrients throughout the plant. The veins running through a plant's leaves are a visible part of the vascular system. It is the equivalent of the circulatory system in animals. There are two types of tissue involved in the vascular system—**xylem** and **phloem**. Xylem and phloem are organized as a network of pipelines running through the plant.

Xylem

Xylem is the plant's water transportation system, moving water and dissolved minerals through the plant. It also provides support. Xylem is mainly composed of two cell types, **tracheids** and **vessel members** (or vessel elements). Both types are long cells that join together in columns along shoots and roots. They have thick cell walls that are strengthened and waterproofed with **lignin**. Once xylem cells have reached full size, they die. The **cytoplasm** of the cell disappears and all that remains is the cell wall.

Tracheids are long, narrow cells with tapering ends.

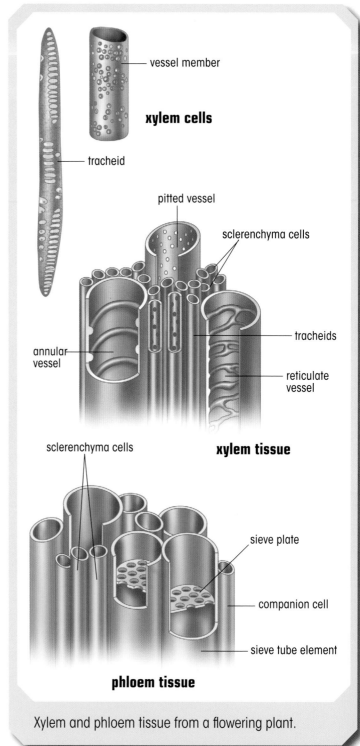

xylem cells

vessel member

tracheid

pitted vessel

sclerenchyma cells

annular vessel

tracheids

reticulate vessel

xylem tissue

sclerenchyma cells

sieve plate

companion cell

sieve tube element

phloem tissue

Xylem and phloem tissue from a flowering plant.

The cell walls are dotted with tiny holes called pits, which allow water to flow in and out of the cells along the xylem. Vessel members are wider than tracheids and are only found in flowering plants. As vessel cells develop, their outer walls connect to form rigid pipelines through the plant. Where two cells meet, the end walls are at first perforated with holes and eventually disappear altogether. These vessel tubes conduct water much better than the narrow tracheids.

Phloem

Phloem carries sugars and other dissolved nutrients around the plant. Like xylem, it consists mainly of two types of cells. These are called **sieve tube members** and **companion cells**. Both types have very thin walls, unlike the thick-walled xylem cells. Also, unlike xylem cells, the phloem cells do not die when they are fully grown. This is because moving nutrients throughout the plant is an active process. Phloem cells must use energy to move sugars and other nutrients through the system.

Sieve tube members are the main cells through which nutrients are transported in the plant. Sieve cells are joined together at their ends. But unlike xylem tubes, the ends of the cells do not disappear. Instead, they contain a number of holes, which line up with corresponding holes in the next cell. These perforated end walls are called **sieve plates**. Mature sieve cells lose their **nucleus**.

You might wonder how sieve cells get the instructions they need to work properly without a nucleus. Under the microscope, it can be seen that at least one companion cell is associated with each sieve cell. Companion cells keep their nucleus, and it is believed that one of the functions of the companion cell is to provide genetic information for itself and its sieve cell sister.

The bark of this maritime pine tree (*Pinus pinaster*) has been tapped for its resinous sap, which will be turned into turpentine. The tree's phloem tissue, which carries the sap, is just beneath the bark.

The Epidermis

The outer surfaces of a plant are protected by a layer of cells called the **epidermis**. These nonspecialized cells are tightly packed together, and most have no **chloroplasts**. Waxes and a fatty substance called cutin cover the outer surfaces of the cells, forming a protective coat called a **cuticle**.

This outermost layer of cells is very important to the plant's well-being. The cuticle helps prevent water loss from the plant and also helps protect from attack by micro-organisms. It is also transparent, which allows light to reach the photosynthetic **tissues** within the plant.

Stomata

The epidermis is not a continuous, unbroken sheet of cells. If it was, the plant would suffocate and die. The surface of the plant's stems and leaves is dotted with tiny openings called **stomata**.

Plants, like most living things, require a continuous supply of oxygen. Oxygen is an essential ingredient for **respiration**, the process by which living things break down nutrients from food to get energy. During respiration, oxygen is absorbed by the cells and carbon dioxide is produced as waste. Plants also need carbon dioxide from the air, which is used in **photosynthesis**. Photosynthesis uses up carbon dioxide and produces oxygen as waste.

In the hours of daylight, the rate of photosynthesis far exceeds that of respiration, and the plant is takes in carbon dioxide and gives off oxygen. At night there is no photosynthesis, so the plant takes in oxygen and gives off carbon dioxide. This constant flow of gases takes place through the stomata.

Plants such as geraniums (*Geranium* species) have hairs in the epidermal layer of cells that provide additional protection against insects.

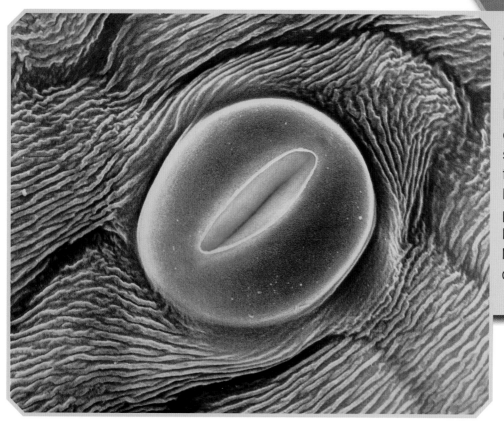

A single stoma. One leaf may have a million or more stomata, but these openings are so small that they make up less than one percent of the leaf's surface. Magnification approx. x 1,000.

Transpiration

Most of the water a plant takes up through its roots is lost through the stomata. The loss of moisture from the leaves and other plant parts is called **transpiration**. Transpiration provides the force that keeps water flowing up from the roots to the leaves. Water forms a continuous column as it flows from the roots, through the stem, and into the leaves. As water is lost through evaporation, the entire column of water is pulled upward and more water is pulled in through the roots. Transpiration is strong enough to draw water to the top of a 300-foot tree.

There are thousands of stomata on every square inch of a leaf. In most plants the stomata are open during the day, when photosynthesis takes place, so that the carbon dioxide the plant needs can get in.

Around each stoma there are a pair of specialized cells called **guard cells**. When these guard cells take in water from epidermal cells around them, they swell up. This makes them bend in such a way that an opening forms between them. When the guard cells lose water they collapse against each other, closing the gap once more.

Guard cells are the only cells in the epidermis that contain chloroplasts. These chloroplasts are an important part of the mechanism by which the stomata open and close. During the hours of daylight, the chloroplasts in the guard cells photosynthesize and use up carbon dioxide. The low carbon dioxide levels trigger a process that results in water flowing into the cells, and the stoma opens. At night photosynthesis stops, and the carbon dioxide levels in the guard cells rise again. This sets off a flow of water out of the guard cells, which collapse and close the stoma.

4 | Stems

The stem is the part of a plant that produces and supports all of the above ground parts of the plant: the buds, leaves, flowers, and fruit. The stem is the main pipeline that carries water and dissolved **minerals** from the roots and sugars manufactured in the leaves to other parts of the plant. In many plants the stem ensures that the leaves are spread to effectively gather sunlight for **photosynthesis**. A few types of stems grow underground or horizontally along the ground.

All seed-bearing plants (the **angiosperms** and the **gymnosperms**) have stems. Simpler plants such as liverworts, hornworts, and mosses, do not. Plant stems vary greatly in size and appearance from one species to another. A cauliflower has a short, stubby stem, for example, whereas the trunk of a tree is a huge stem that in some species can be more than 300 feet long.

Buds

The plant stem produces buds from which new shoots, leaves, and flowers grow. The bud is often protected by a cluster of modified leaves, called bud scales. Bud scales prevent water loss and protect the delicate growing **tissues** of the bud. Buds develop on the stem at points called nodes, in the upper angle where leaves attach to the stem. Many plants have a shoot tip, or terminal bud, at the end of each shoot. This growing point is an apical **meristem**. As the stem grows, plant tissues beneath the apical meristem become gradually more specialized, and **differentiate** to form new leaves, flowers, and stems.

Herbaceous and woody stems

Herbaceous plants are those without woody stems, such as grasses and daisies. Herbaceous stems have soft tissues and grow very little in diameter. Most plants with herbaceous stems are annuals, living for only one growing season. Herbaceous stems consist mainly of primary tissues that develop from the apical meristem.

A tree's bark protects it from many types of injury, but some insects can cause serious damage. Bark beetles (family Scolytidae) bore galleries beneath the bark, where they lay their eggs. A bad infestation of these beetles can kill a tree. Magnification approx. x 23.

Trees and shrubs have tough woody stems. Each growing season, woody stems develop new tissues that cause them to grow in diameter. The new layers form the annual rings visible in the trunk of a tree that has been cut down.

During their first year of growth, woody stems begin to develop secondary tissues. These support or replace primary tissues by producing wood and bark. As the stem grows wider, the **epidermis** breaks apart and falls away.

In woody stems, bark replaces the epidermis as a protective covering. The bark is made up of a hard, dense tissue called cork. Cork insulates, waterproofs, and protects the stem. It also forms over wounds in the stem, like a scab forming over injured skin. Only the innermost cells of the cork layer remain alive, because only they have access to the nutrients carried by the **phloem** and **xylem**. The older outer bark gradually wears away or splits apart and falls off as the stem grows wider.

Specialized stems

Some stems perform special functions. Bulbs and tubers, for example, are underground stems that can store large amounts of food. A bulb is a short stem surrounded by fleshy leaves. Onions are bulbs. Tubers are short and swollen and grow underground at the tip of the stems of plants such as potatoes.

Runners are specialized stems that are active in reproduction. Runners grow along the ground and produce new plants. Strawberries are examples of plants that spread by way of runners.

Some varieties of onion (*Allium cepa*).

Looking at Leaves

A plant's leaves are its food factories. They are designed to gather energy from sunlight, then use this energy to make food (sugars). The sugars provide the plant with the energy and materials it needs to grow and to produce flowers and seeds.

Leaf parts

Most leaves have two main parts: the blade, or lamina, and the **petiole**, or leafstalk. The broad, flat part of the leaf is called the blade, and this is where **photosynthesis** takes place.

The leaf blade is usually less than 0.04 inches (1 millimeter) thick. Such a thin, flat structure would fold up if it were not strengthened in some way. Running through the blade is a network of veins; these bundles of **phloem** and **xylem** cells transport water and nutrients through the leaf. They are tougher and stronger than the **tissue** around them and prevent the leaf from collapsing or tearing.

The petiole is the stemlike part of the leaf. The veins run into the petiole, attaching the leaf to the rest of the plant. In some plants, the petiole is very thick: a stick of celery is a petiole, for instance. By contrast, plants such as grasses have no petioles.

In many plants, the petioles can bend and twist to move the leaf blades into the best position for gathering sunlight. You can actually see the leaves moving to follow the sun through the course of a day.

A typical leaf is broad and oval-shaped, but there are many other leaf shapes.

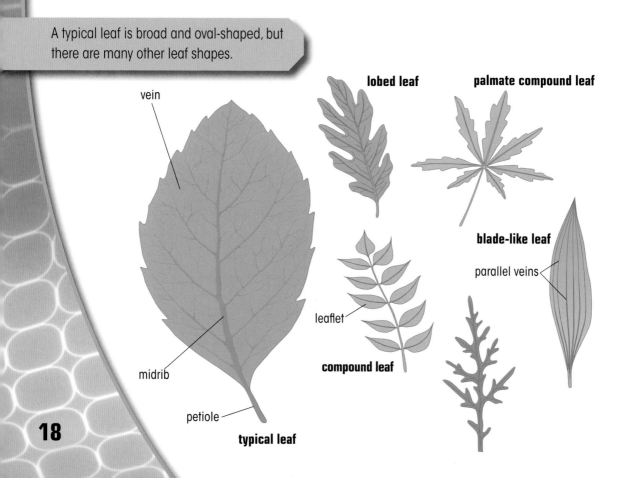

lobed leaf

palmate compound leaf

vein

blade-like leaf

parallel veins

leaflet

compound leaf

midrib

petiole

typical leaf

A tree's leaves spread in a wide canopy to catch the maximum amount of sunlight. The leaves are arranged so that they overlap as little as possible.

As in the rest of the plant, the outer surface of the leaf is covered with a waxy **cuticle**. In plants that grow in bright sunlight, this cuticle is often very thick. This helps to filter out strong light and keeps water loss to a minimum. The leaves may also have tiny hairlike projections that reduce the effects of bright light. Plants that grow in the shade have a very thin cuticle, to allow in as much light as possible.

Leaf shape

Leaves vary widely in their size and shape. A duckweed leaf may be no more than 0.04 inches (1 millimeter) across, while a water lily's leaves may measure 7 feet (2.1 meters) or more. Many are oval, but others are shaped like arrowheads, feathers, hearts, spikes, and tubes. Leaves can be broadly divided into three groups according to their basic shape.

- leaves are fairly wide and flat. This is the type of leaf that most **dicot** plants have, including oak trees, pea plants, and roses.

- leaves are long and slender. They are found on many **monocot** plants such as onions, lilies, and grasses such as barley, oats, wheat, and corn.

- leaves are short, thick, and needle-like. They are typical of firs, pines, cedars, and other **conifers**.

Whatever their size or shape, most leaves are thin. This gives them a large surface area relative to their size for gathering sunlight.

Inside the Food Factory

We have seen how the overall design of a leaf is adapted for **photosynthesis**. Under a microscope, it is possible to see how the inside of the leaf is designed to get the most out of the available light.

Photosynthesizing cells

Most leaves are only a few layers of cells thick. This means that even the cells on the shady side of the leaf get some light. The leaves of **dicots** have an upper and a lower surface: the upper side always faces the light, while the lower side is in shade. This is reflected in the leaf's structure.

The top surface of the leaf is a single layer of transparent **epidermis** cells. Immediately below this are the cells in which most photosynthesis takes place. These are slender, column-shaped cells, packed with **chloroplasts**, called the palisade **mesophyll**. Below this is a layer of larger, irregular-shaped cells called the spongy mesophyll. Large air spaces between the spongy mesophyll cells connect with the **stomata** on the leaf surface. They allow carbon dioxide to reach the cells easily and quickly, and oxygen to escape. The spongy mesophyll cells have fewer chloroplasts than palisade mesophyll cells, but they still photosynthesize.

In the leaves of **monocot** plants such as grasses, the palisade and spongy mesophyll are not organized into two layers. This is because the leaves grow vertically, so light falls on them from all directions.

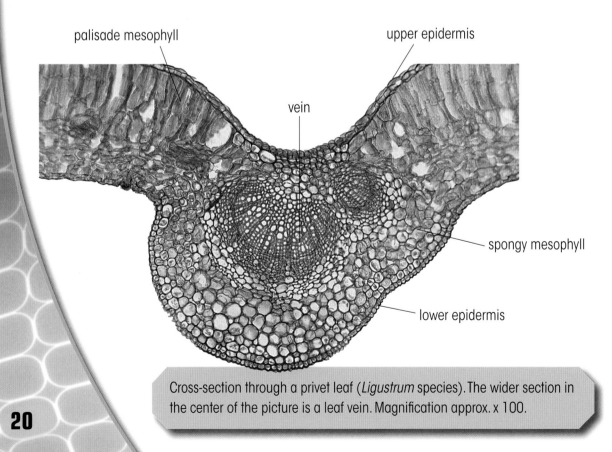

palisade mesophyll

upper epidermis

vein

spongy mesophyll

lower epidermis

Cross-section through a privet leaf (*Ligustrum* species). The wider section in the center of the picture is a leaf vein. Magnification approx. x 100.

The colors of the fall leaves on these trees in Maine range from brown through bright red to pale yellow.

Fall colors

A leaf is green because of the **chlorophyll** it contains. During the growing season a leaf becomes tougher as its cells develop thicker walls, and changes color from bright green to a duller green. In the leaves of **deciduous** trees and shrubs (plants that lose their leaves in the fall), a corky layer of cells known as the **abscission zone** develops where the stalk of the leaf joins the stem. As fall approaches, the shorter days and cooler nights cause the chlorophyll in the leaves to break down. As this happens, yellow and orange-red pigments in the leaf that had been hidden by the green of the chlorophyll are revealed. A group of red and purple pigments also forms in the dying leaf. After the chlorophyll breaks down, the leaf can no longer make food. The cells in the abscission zone separate or dissolve, and the leaf falls from the tree.

Leaf Specializations

Some plant leaves have other functions as well as, or instead of, food-making. Such specializations include protection, storage, support, and food capture.

These sweet peas (*Lathyrus odoratus*) have some leaves adapted as tendrils for climbing, and some leaves for photosynthesis.

Protective leaves

Leaves that are specialized to protect the plant include bud scales, prickles, and spines. We have already seen that bud scales protect the young, delicate **tissues** of growing buds. Prickles and spines are sharp leaf structures that discourage animals from eating the plant. For instance, prickles cover the leaves of the thistle and protect the plant from grazing animals. The clusters of sharp spines on many cacti are specialized leaves that not only offer protection but also cut down on water loss in the desert. In a cactus, the green stem of the plant takes over the task of **photosynthesis** from the leaves.

Storage leaves

Most plants store food in their roots or stems. However, some plants have special leaves that hold extra food. Onion and tulip bulbs, for example, consist mainly of short, fat storage leaves called bulb scales. These leaves have no **chloroplasts** and cannot make food. Their role is to store food underground during the winter to provide the energy for new growth in the spring.

Many plants that grow in dry places have thick leaves that store water and look fleshy or swollen. These plants are called **succulents**. They include house leeks, stonecrops, and strange plants called "living stones" (*Lithops* species) that look like stones. The **cuticle** of succulent plants has a waxy coating. They have fewer **stomata** than other plants and the stomata are sunk into pits in the cuticle to prevent water loss. The stomata never open during the day and during periods of drought can remain closed altogether.

Support leaves

Many climbing plants have leaves that become slender, whiplike structures called tendrils. These wrap around twigs, wires, and other solid objects to help support the plant. For example, climbing garden peas have divided leaves in which the upper leaflets are threadlike tendrils. In one type of sweet pea, the entire leaf blade becomes a tendril.

The floating leaves of a water lily have very little cuticle, since water conservation is not a problem. The **mesophyll** has large air spaces, especially around the **vascular** bundles. The air trapped there acts like water wings and helps to keep the leaf afloat. This specialized mesophyll is often called aerenchyma.

Bracts

Bracts are leaflike structures that grow just below the flowers of certain plants. Most bracts are generally smaller and simpler in shape than the true leaves. Many members of the daisy family, such as daisies, marigolds, and sunflowers, have bracts that form a cup beneath the plant's cluster of flowers. In some plants, such as the poinsettia and flowering dogwood, the bracts are brightly colored and take on the role of attracting pollinating insects to the small-**petalled** flowers.

Insect-capturing leaves

Plants such as the butterwort, pitcher plant, sundew, and Venus flytrap grow in wetlands, where the soil contains little nitrogen. To get the nitrogen they need, these plants "eat" insects. The leaves of these plants are specialized to attract, trap, and digest insects. The Venus flytrap, for example, has a leaf that is divided in two, with a hinge down the middle. If an insect lands on the leaf, the two sides suddenly close together and trap it. Curved spines around the edge of the leaf keep the insect from escaping.

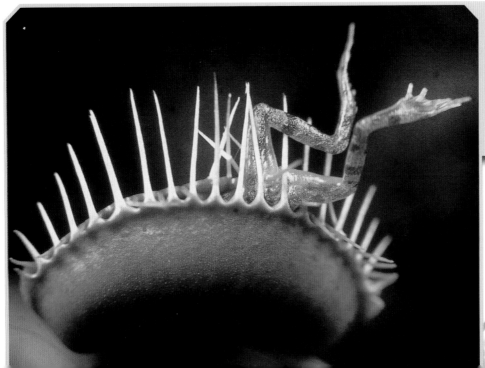

This Venus fly-trap (*Dionaea* species) has caught an unusual victim— a young frog.

When a plant seed begins to grow, the first thing to emerge is the primary root. The roots absorb water from the soil, along with essential elements such as nitrogen and **minerals**. Minerals are simple chemicals containing calcium, magnesium, and phosphorus. These elements and minerals are essential parts of important plant chemicals. Nitrogen, for instance, is found in **proteins** and DNA, while magnesium is a part of the **chlorophyll molecule**. The plant's **vascular system** carries the water and minerals to all parts of the plant.

Hidden from sight beneath the ground, the **root system** can spread out over a large area. This branching network of roots anchors the plant. More importantly, it gives a large surface area for absorbing materials from the soil.

Root systems

The root systems of **dicot** and **monocot** plants grow in different ways. In dicot plants such as oak trees and carrots, the primary root grows downward into the soil and gets thicker as it grows. Lateral roots then begin to branch off from the primary root. A primary root, together with its lateral branches, forms a **tap root system**.

Monocot plant roots grow differently. The primary root of a monocot plant, such as wheat or an orchid, is short-lived. Roots grow from the plant stem to take its place and lateral roots branch from these new roots. The lateral roots are all roughly the same length and diameter. Roots formed in this way together make a **fibrous root system**.

The tap root system of a typical dicot plant (a), the fibrous roots of a typical monocot (b) and an enlarged view of a root tip (c).

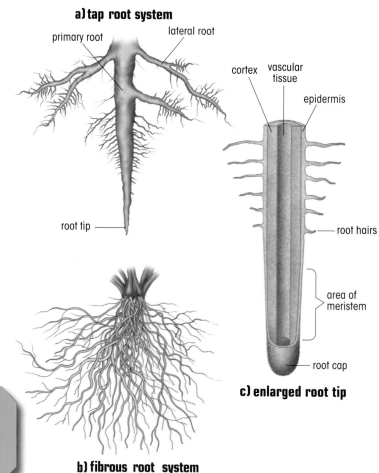

a) tap root system

primary root — lateral root

cortex — vascular tissue — epidermis

root tip

root hairs

area of meristem

root cap

c) enlarged root tip

b) fibrous root system

Roots at work

At the tip of each root a dome-shaped cap protects the **meristem**, where cell division takes place. The root **epidermis** is where absorption of water and minerals from the soil takes place.

Most of this absorption occurs near the tips of roots, through root hairs, which are fine extensions of the epidermal cells. A plant can have billions of root hairs. The hairs cling tightly to soil particles and provide a huge surface area through which water and minerals can be absorbed.

Cell membranes allow water, oxygen, and carbon dioxide to pass freely, but keep other substances, such as salts, from passing through. When two solutions are separated by a cell membrane (or any other partially permeable membrane), water flows from the solution of lowest concentration toward the solution of highest concentration. This process is known as **osmosis**. In the roots, the concentration of salts in the root hairs is greater than in the surrounding soil, so water flows from the soil into the roots. The root hairs of a mature corn plant absorb more than 3 quarts (2.8 liters) of water every day.

Instead of using a bulb for food storage, a carrot (*Daucus carota*) uses an enlarged fleshy root.

Some minerals are drawn passively into the roots along with the water. Others enter by simple **diffusion**. The plant can also take in minerals by active transport. This involves special proteins that pump minerals across the cell membranes. Active transportation allows the plant to move minerals into the roots that would otherwise stay in the soil, but the root cells have to use energy to make it happen.

The endodermis

Water and minerals absorbed by the root hairs flow into the center of the root, where the transportation **tissues** are situated. Surrounding the **vascular tissue** at the center of the root is a layer of cells called the endodermis. Like in all cells, the membranes of endodermal cells let some substances into the cell but not others. They act like a guard post for the plant, controlling the amount and type of material that enters the plant's transportation system from the soil.

Sexual Reproduction

Flowers are the reproductive organs of flowering plants. They develop from buds along the stem of a plant. Some plants have only a single flower, while others grow many large clusters of flowers. Plants such as dandelions and daisies have many tiny flowers that form a single, flower-like head.

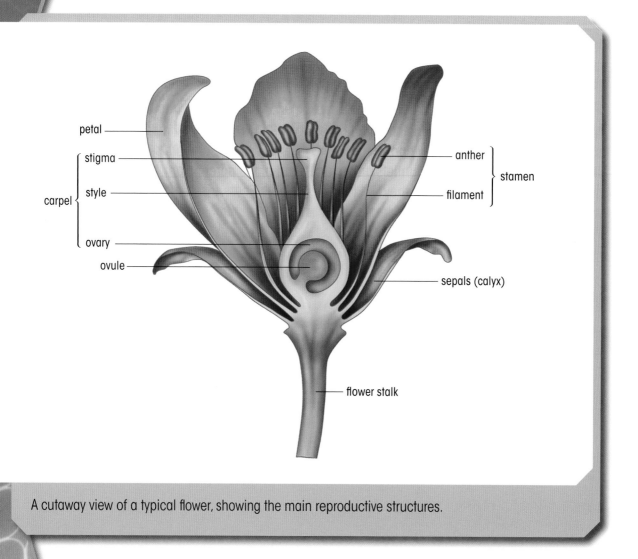

A cutaway view of a typical flower, showing the main reproductive structures.

Most flowers have four main parts:

- the calyx is made up of small, usually green, leaflike structures called **sepals**, which protect the bud of a young flower
- the corolla, the **petals** of the flower, is usually the largest, most colorful part of the flower
- **stamens** are the male reproductive part of the flower
- **carpels** are the female reproductive part of the flower.

Sepals and petals

Like leaves, sepals and petals are made up of **ground tissue**, **vascular tissue**, and **epidermis**. Some of the epidermal cells in a petal produce fragrant oils. This is what gives many flowers a pleasant smell. Cells of the ground tissue frequently contain pigments that give the petals their bright colors. Small, light-reflecting crystals may also be present. This show of sight and smell, pleasant though it may be, is not for our benefit. Its purpose is to attract pollinators.

There is a large variety of garden flowers, but these form only a small part of the much wider variety of flowering plants.

Stamens and carpels

The stamens and the carpels are found inside the sepals and the petals. In many flowers, the stamens and petals are joined together. Each stamen has a long, narrow stalk called a filament, on the end of which there is an enlarged part called an **anther**. **Pollen** grains, each of which develops into two male sex cells, are produced in the anthers. Many flowers have a single, centrally positioned carpel. Others may have more, perhaps fused together in a compound structure. The carpels of most flowers have three main parts. At the top there is a flattened structure called the **stigma**, a sticky or hairy surface that captures the pollen grains. From this, a slender tube called the **style** extends down to the rounded **ovary** at the base. The ovary contains one or more structures called **ovules**. The ovules are where the egg cells form. In most species of flowering plants, one spore in each ovule develops into an egg cell. When sperm cells fertilize the egg cells, seeds form.

Separate flowers

Some species of plants produce flowers that have both male and female parts. These are called perfect flowers. Flowers that contain only male or female parts are called imperfect flowers. In plants such as oaks, a single plant can have both male and female flowers. In other plants, such as the willow, male and female flowers are on separate plants.

Pollination and Fertilization

Every spring, the **anthers** of flowering plants release large quantities of **pollen**. For fertilization to take place, a pollen grain must be transferred from the male to the female parts of the flower. This transfer is called **pollination**. Some plants pollinate their own flowers. Pollen from a flower reaches a **carpel** of the same flower, or a carpel of another flower on the same plant. This process is called self-pollination. Other plants need to have pollen from another plant of the same species for fertilization to take place. This is called cross-pollination and requires the services of a pollinator.

A pollinator is anything that transfers pollen from the male reproductive parts of one flower to the female reproductive parts of another. Pollen grains can be carried from flower to flower by wind or water. Plants that are wind-pollinated have long anthers that produce large amounts of very light pollen that can be carried for long distances on the wind. Wind-pollinated flowers are often small and inconspicuous with tiny **petals** or no petals at all. Many types of tree and grass are wind-pollinated. The water-dwelling ribbon weed releases tiny free-floating flowers, called pollen boats. These drift across the surface of the water, and with luck they will bump into a female flower before they are swallowed by a fish!

Flowers and animals

Many cross-pollinated plants have large flowers, a sweet scent, and sweet nectar. These features attract birds, bats, and insects such as ants, bees, beetles, butterflies, and moths. As these animals move from flower to flower in search of food, they carry pollen on their bodies.

One of the most important partnerships in all of nature is that between flowering plants and insects. Over the course of millions of years, plants and their pollinators have adapted to each other. At first, all flowering

A long-tongued bat (*Glossophaga sorciina*) feeding on a flower. The long tongue of this bat is ideal for reaching nectar. These bats are important pollinators.

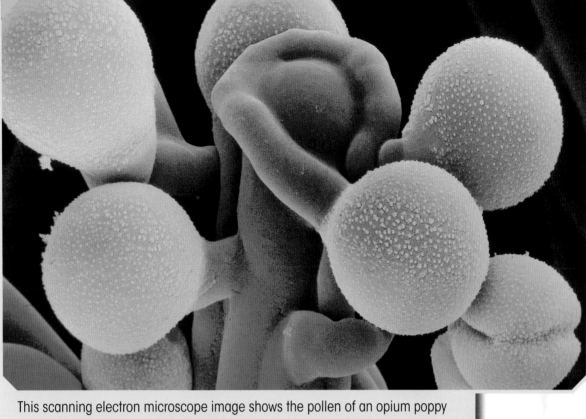

This scanning electron microscope image shows the pollen of an opium poppy (*Papaver somniferum*) clustered around part of the stigma. Pollen tubes can be seen growing from many of the grains. Magnification approx. x 650.

plants would have been pollinated randomly by wind and water. However, when insects began to exploit the nutritious qualities of pollen they accidentally made more accurate deliveries of pollen from flower to flower as they searched for food. The plant might have lost some pollen to the insects but it gained a great advantage over its competitor plants because it successfully formed more seeds.

We can see examples all around us of the way plants and their pollinators have evolved together. Sweet-smelling flowers with light-colored petals, such as evening primrose and some tobacco plants, attract moths and bats in the evening. Red and yellow flowers of many tropical plants attract birds such as hummingbirds, which can see well but have no sense of smell. In Australia there are more than a thousand flower species that are pollinated by birds. Then there are flowers such as Rafflesia, the largest flowers in the world, that smell like rotten meat and are pollinated by flies and beetles.

Fertilization

If a pollen grain successfully reaches a carpel it starts to grow and develop into a tubular structure. This pollen tube grows down, carrying the sperm **nuclei** with it, through the **stigma** and the **style** to an **ovule** in the **ovary**. When the pollen tube reaches the ovule it ruptures and releases its two nuclei. One nucleus unites with the nucleus of the egg cell and a new plant embryo begins to form. The second nucleus unites with another cell in the ovule and begins to develop into a food store for the new embryo. The plant embryo and its food store together form the seed.

Seeds and Germination

Seeds vary greatly in size and shape. Some, such as those of the tobacco plant, are so small that 2,500 of them fit into a pod less than 1 inch (2.5 centimeters) long. At the other end of the scale, the seeds of one kind of coconut tree may weigh more than 20 pounds (9 kilograms). However, the size of the seed tells us little about the size of the plant that may grow from it. For example, giant sequoias grow from seeds that are less than 0.08 inches (2 millimeters) long.

The parts of a seed

Seeds consist of three main parts: the seed coat, the food storage **tissue**, and the embryo. The seed coat protects the embryo, which contains all the parts needed to form a new plant.

In flowering plants, the food storage tissue is called the **endosperm**. It contains large amounts of energy storage substances, such as starch, plus smaller amounts of **proteins** and other nutrients.

The embryo is the part of the seed that will grow into a new plant. The embryo has either one or two **cotyledons**, or embryo leaves (one if it is a **monocot** and two if it is a **dicot**). These cotyledons absorb food from the food storage tissue.

A ripe pomegranate (*Punica granatum*) is tasty to eat, but its flesh is full of seeds. If the pomegranate is eaten, some seeds survive the journey through the stomach and grow in the animal's droppings.

Forming fruits

In all flowering plants, the seeds are enclosed by an **ovary**. As the seeds mature, the ovary develops into a fruit. Oranges, lemons, grapes, and other fruits that we eat are only one kind of plant fruit. Pea and bean pods are also fruits, as are dandelion's fluffy parachutes and the winged "helicopters" of trees such as maples.

The purpose of these fruits is to protect the seeds until they are mature, then to spread the seeds as widely as possible. Some fruits burst as they dry out, catapulting the seeds away from the plant. Wings and parachutes help a seed to be carried by the wind. Many of the fruits that we eat have evolved to be eaten by animals. These seeds pass unharmed through the animal's digestive tract, and are deposited perhaps miles from the parent plant in the animal's droppings.

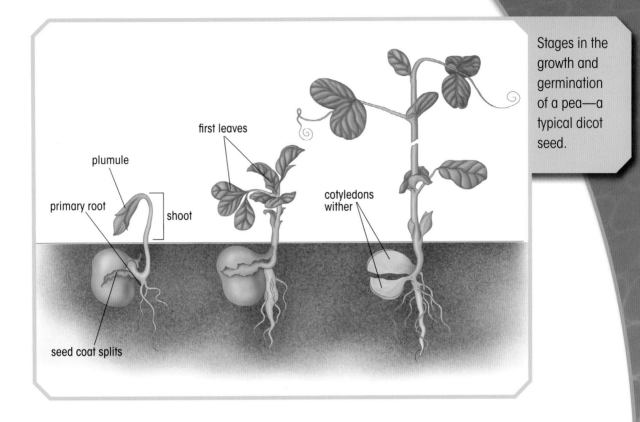

Labels in the diagram: first leaves, plumule, primary root, shoot, cotyledons wither, seed coat splits

Germination

The sprouting of a seed is called **germination**. Most seeds go through a period of inactivity called **dormancy** before they start to grow. In many parts of the world, this period lasts through the winter. Then, when spring arrives, the seeds start to germinate.

Seeds rely on environmental factors such as temperature, moisture, and oxygen levels in the soil to trigger their germination. Most seeds, like most kinds of plants, grow best in a temperature between 64 °F (18 °C) and 84 °F (29 °C). They also need just the right amount of moisture. Moisture softens the seed coat, allowing the growing parts to break through. If there is too much water, the seed can begin to rot, while with too little water germination may take place slowly or not at all.

Seeds also need oxygen for germination. To grow, the seed embryo needs energy. It gets this energy from its food store, by the process of **respiration**. Without oxygen, respiration is much less efficient, and produces little energy.

From seed to seedling

The first structure to develop from the germinating seed is the primary root, or **radicle**. The root is important because the one thing not stored in the seed is water, which the germinating seed must get from the soil. Once the root is growing, a shoot begins to develop from the upper part of the seedling. At the tip of the growing shoot is the **plumule**, the bud that produces the first leaves. Until the seedling's first leaves begin to grow, its cotyledons are its main source of food. Once the seedling has developed roots and leaves, and has begun to produce its own food, the cotyledons wither away.

Spores and Cones

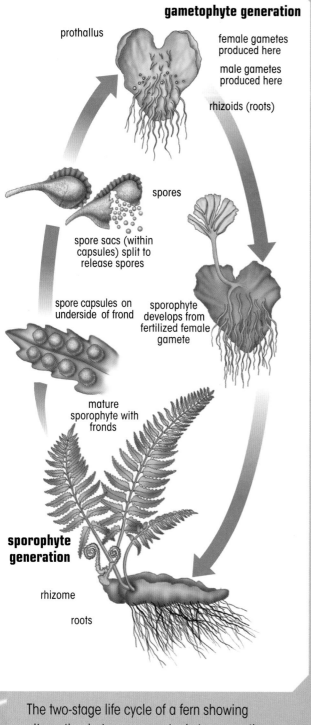

gametophyte generation

prothallus

female gametes produced here

male gametes produced here

rhizoids (roots)

spores

spore sacs (within capsules) split to release spores

spore capsules on underside of frond

sporophyte develops from fertilized female gamete

mature sporophyte with fronds

sporophyte generation

rhizome

roots

The two-stage life cycle of a fern showing alternation between gametophyte generation and sporophyte generation.

Some plants do not produce flowers and seeds. The seeds of **gymnosperms** develop in scaly cones. In some plant life cycles there are two distinct forms of the plant, occurring alternately. This is called alternation of generations.

Mosses and ferns

Mosses and ferns are examples of alternation of generation. They go through a two-stage life cycle. One stage, called the **gametophyte** generation, is the one during which the plant produces its sex cells, or **gametes**. Mosses in the gametophyte stage are the small green plants we are familiar with. In a clump of moss there will be male and female gametophytes. At the tip of each gametophyte eggs and sperm develop according to the sex of the plant. The male gametes have whip-like tails called flagella. They use these to move through the film of water on the plants to reach the eggs on the female gametophytes.

The next stage of development after fertilization is the sporophyte generation. A long, thin stalk grows up from the fertilized gametophyte. At the top of the stalk there is a podlike, spore-producing container. Inside there are thousands of single-celled spores. When these are released from the pod they germinate and grow. Some develop into male gametophytes and some into female gametophytes. The cycle begins again.

Ferns also go through a two-stage cycle. The fern plant we normally see is the sporophyte generation. If you look on the underside of a fern leaf you may see clusters of sporangia, or spore capsules. After the spores ripen they fall from the sporangia to the ground, where they germinate and grow into tiny heart-shaped gametophytes.

Fern gametophytes produce both male and female gametes. A new sporophyte will grow from the fertilized gametophyte. The next generation begins.

Gymnosperms

Gymnosperms, such as the **conifers**, do not have flowers. Their reproductive parts are in cones. A conifer plant has two types of cones. The **pollen** cone, or male cone, is simpler in structure and is the smaller and softer of the two. Light, powdery pollen grains are produced here. The seed cone (the female cone) is larger and harder than the male cone. Each of the scales that make up a seed cone has two **ovules** on its surface.

Pollen grains are released from the pollen cone and carried on the wind to the seed cone. Sticky surfaces near each ovule trap pollen grains, which then enter the ovule's pollen chamber. The pollen grain then begins to form a pollen tube. Once the pollen tube reaches the egg cell, it releases its two **nuclei**. One of the two nuclei fertilizes the egg. The other nucleus simply disintegrates: it does not help to form a food reserve for the new plant like in flowering plants. The fertilized egg develops into an embryo, and the ovule containing the embryo becomes a seed.

Male and female cones of the bristlecone pine (*Pinus aristata*). The small, red cone on the lower right is the male cone; the large cone in the center is the female seed cone.

The word *gymnosperm* means naked or uncovered seed. Gymnosperms have this name because their seeds are not enclosed inside fruits. Once the seeds are mature, the cone releases its seeds. The seeds fall to the ground and, if conditions are favorable, new plants begin to grow.

Ancient gymnosperms

Today there are only a few kinds of gymnosperm—roughly 750 conifer species, a handful of cycads (plants with a stout trunk and crown of large leaves), and a single species of ginkgo tree. In the Jurassic period, roughly 200 million years ago, ginkgoes, conifers, and cycads formed large forests across the world. Cycads were so widespread that the Jurassic period, which we think of as the age of the dinosaurs, is sometimes called the "age of the cycads." When the **angiosperms** appeared, about 140 million years ago, the gymnosperms began to decline.

8 Fungi

Fungi are often mistakenly thought of as plants. But they are very different and have their own place in the living world—the fungi kingdom. Fungi include familiar species such as mushrooms, puffballs, and toadstools, as well as less obvious organisms such as yeasts and the molds that grow on stale food.

Looking at fungi

Unlike plants, fungi do not **photosynthesize** so they cannot make their own food. Instead, like animals, they must get their nutrients from organic matter. Like all other living things except **archaea** and bacteria, fungi are **eukaryotes**.

World's biggest fungus?

A fungus was found stretching over an area of 96 million square feet (8.9 million square meters) in a forest in eastern Oregon. At its widest it is 3.5 miles (5.6 kilometers) across. Experts estimate that it could be up to 7,000 years old.

Fungal cells have walls, like a plant cell. This cell wall may contain cellulose, as in plant cell walls. But most fungal cell walls also contain chitin, a substance similar to cellulose that is also found in the hard outer skeletons of insects and spiders. This difference between fungal and plant cell walls allows fungi to play an important role in the living world, as we shall see.

Parchment mushrooms (*Stereum complicatum*) are a type of bracket fungus. They have enzymes that enable them to obtain nutrients from living and dead wood.

This photo, taken with a scanning electron microscope, shows part of the mycelium of three *Drechslera* fungus species. The mass of threads that fill the picture are hyphae. This type of fungus grows on grass and cereals.

Although there are some single-celled species (such as yeasts), most fungi are made up of cells that form thin, microscopic filaments called **hyphae**. A network of hyphae together forms a **mycelium**, the body of a fungus. The hyphae form a complex system of microscopic tubes lined with **cytoplasm**.

Fungal feeding

Some fungi feed on dead and decaying animals or plants; others are parasites, feeding on living plants or animals, including humans. Growing fungal hyphae produce **enzymes** that digest their food outside the body of the fungus. The fungus then absorbs the products of this digestion. Fungi that attack plants can produce enzymes that break down the cellulose cell walls of the plant cells, but have no effect on the chitin walls of the fungus.

Decomposers

Most fungi live on dead organic matter. Along with the bacteria, these fungi are the living world's clean-up squad. By breaking down once-living material, the fungi release valuable raw materials, such as carbon dioxide, nitrogen, and other elements for recycling through the ecosystem. The nutrients released by these fungal decomposers return to the soil, where they can be absorbed once again by plants. Many fungi also help to maintain soil structure. They produce glue-like substances that attach soil particles together. This creates pores in the soil that allow air and water to filter through and reach plant roots.

Because fungi are such active decomposers, they might be seen as agents of destruction. For example, dry rot, which is a type of fungus, can cause a great deal of damage in buildings. However, in its natural setting the fungus plays a vital role in recycling the dead trees in forests. The cellulose-destroying enzymes allow fungi to attack all types of plant material, even wood. Without them and other decomposers, there would soon be no space for new trees to grow.

39

Spores, More Spores, and Buds

The mushrooms and toadstools you see growing from the ground are not whole fungi. They are the above-ground parts of a **mycelium** buried in the soil that could stretch far beneath your feet. Mushrooms are the reproductive organs of a fungus.

A portion of the fungal **hyphae** weave together to form the mushrooms that we see. Look at one closely and you will see that it has a stipe, or stalk, and a cap. The underside of the cap is lined with gills, fine sheets of **tissue**, and the fungus produces spores on the gills. Each spore contains a little **cytoplasm** and one or more **nuclei**, depending on the species of fungus. These spores are the reproductive cells of the fungus. Fungi reproduce by producing spores in large numbers.

Mold fungi, such as those you can see growing on moldy bread, do not produce mushrooms. Instead they send up vertical hyphae from the mycelium. Chains of spores are produced at the tips of these hyphae, giving the fungus a blue-green, powdery appearance.

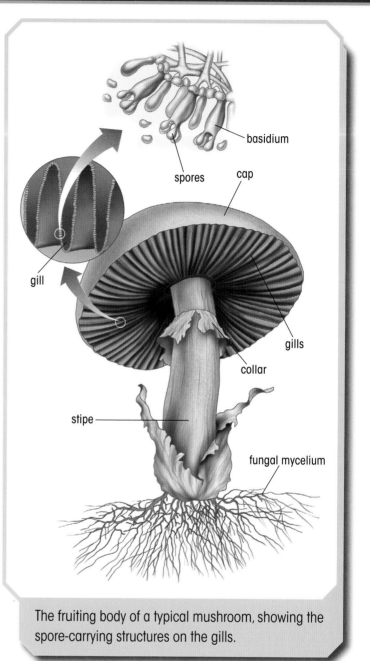

The fruiting body of a typical mushroom, showing the spore-carrying structures on the gills.

Warning: poison!

A few kinds of fungi found in the wild are safe to eat. But many more fungi may make you ill and some are highly poisonous. It is very difficult to tell poisonous and non-poisonous species apart. Never eat a wild fungus unless identified as safe by an expert.

Apples infested with brown rot fungus (*Sclerotina fructigena*). In winter these fungi form a structure called a sclerotium, which consists of a small number of fungal cells inside a tough outer coating. The sclerotium can survive extreme conditions, and then produce a new fruiting body in the spring.

Spore prints

Spore color is an important indicator when trying to identify a fungus. One way to find the color of a mushroom's spores is to take a spore print. Making spore prints is easy. Simply cut the stem off a mushroom, and place the cap half on a piece of white paper, and half on black paper (the two colors of paper are needed in case the mushroom has white spores). Put a bowl over the whole thing and leave it for several hours. Now remove the bowl and carefully pick up the cap. You should have a pattern of spores on the paper that exactly matches the gill pattern of the mushroom. Mushrooms that look similar can have very different spore colors, so this is a very good aid for identifying a species.

Spores are so tiny that they can be carried great distances by air currents. Once the spores land they will germinate, if they are on a suitable source of food. A melon-sized giant puffball can produce 70 billion spores. Each one can potentially give rise to a new mycelium.

Budding

Yeast differs from most fungi in that it consists of single cells. It does not reproduce by means of spores, but by budding. After the cell has reached a certain size it produces a small growth, or bud. The bud gets larger and larger, and eventually breaks away from the parent cell to become a new cell in its own right. On occasion the new cell will start to bud itself before it has separated. This can result in a small chain of linked cells.

Sexual reproduction

Spore production and budding are both forms of **asexual reproduction**. However, most fungi also have a **sexual** means of reproduction at some point in their life cycle. If the hyphae of two fungi of the same species meet, they may fuse together. This can result in fungal cells forming that have a nucleus from each of two different fungi. From this a new mycelium forms that has genetic material from each of the fungi.

Fungal Partnerships

We have already seen how fungi have important relationships with plants, providing them with vital nutrients in the soil. But some fungi live in much closer partnerships with many other organisms.

Two different organisms living together in a close association form a **symbiotic** relationship. Plants and fungi can form such relationships. In some symbiotic relationships one partner gets all the benefit and the other gets nothing, or is actually harmed. The fungal parasites that destroy plant cells are examples of this kind of symbiosis. Some fungi such as blight and mildew are serious plant pests and cause a great deal of damage to crops. There are also a few parasitic fungi that cause diseases in animals.

Lichens (*Eumycota*) on rocks on the Arctic island of Svalbard. Lichens are among the few living things that can grow in these harsh conditions.

Mycorrhizal fungi

Symbiotic partnerships do not have to be destructive: they may be of benefit to both partners. This type of relationship is called **mutualism**. One of the most important fungal relationships is a form of mutualism where plant roots and fungi grow together to form a **mycorrhiza**.

Mycorrhiza means "fungus root," and refers to the mutual relationship between fungi and plant roots, particularly young tree roots. Fungal **hyphae** radiate out through the soil, forming a velvety covering over the roots. Mycorrhizae are commonly found in temperate forests, particularly pine, beech, and birch. They help the trees to withstand seasonal differences in water availability and temperature. Some 5,000 species of fungus enter into these relationships.

In some forms of the relationship the fungal hyphae actually penetrate the plant root cells. The fungus can absorb **minerals** from a larger volume of soil than the plant roots alone and some of these minerals are passed on to the plant. In turn, the fungus absorbs sugars from the root cells. The fungi increases the roots' contact with the soil by 100 to 1,000 times.

Without the benefit of the fungi, plants do not grow as efficiently. Roughly 80 percent of all **vascular plants** form such a relationship, although fewer than 200 species of fungus are known to be involved.

Lichens

Lichens are usually found in places where conditions are too harsh for most organisms. They colonize gateposts and walls, sun-baked rocks, and frozen mountain tops. They are excellent examples of mutualism. In a lichen, a fungus is entwined with **photosynthesizing** micro-organisms called algae. Both grow and reproduce together.

A lichen may be leaflike, flattened, or erect depending on the species involved. The fungus is almost always the largest component of the lichen. The fungus benefits by absorbing a supply of nutrients from the algae. The algae in turn benefit from the shelter they get inside the lichen.

Vital to the Earth

Fungi are not an obvious part of the environment, like plants. But fungal decomposers are important to the soil, and many plants (including whole forests of trees) depend on mycorrhizal fungi for vital nutrients. Unfortunately, many kinds of fungus are sensitive to pollution in the air, and the numbers and variety of fungi are declining.

If pollution deprives trees of their fungal partners, it will damage many forests, perhaps beyond repair. The loss of fungal decomposers would seriously affect the richness of soil. The lives of animals, plants, and fungi are interconnected: damage to one affects them all.

Orchids and fungi

Some types of orchid rely completely on mycorrhizal fungi for their food. These orchids have no **chlorophyll** and cannot photosynthesize. Fungi provide them with all the nutrients they need. Some fungi actually take nutrients from green plants and pass them on to non-photosynthetic ones.

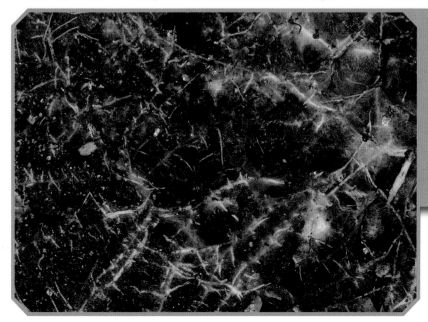

The roots of a lime tree (*Tilia vulgaris*), covered with a white, fluffy covering of mycorrhizal fungus. The hyphae of this type of fungus do not penetrate the root cells. Magnification approx. x 500.

The Plant Kingdom

The plant kingdom consists of multi-celled **eukaryotes**, nearly all of which are **photosynthetic**, though there are a few that are parasites. There are non-vascular as well as vascular species. The vascular species predominate and have well-developed root and shoot systems; nearly all are adapted for life on dry land, though a few are adapted to water environments. They mainly reproduce sexually, though **asexual reproduction** by vegetative propagation, for example, is also common.

Classification	Features	Examples
Phylum Charophyta	seedless, non vascular	
Phylum Bryophyta (**bryophytes**)	seedless, non vascular	mosses, liverworts, hornworts
Phylum Psilophyta	seedless, vascular, no obvious roots or leaves	whisk ferns
Phylum Lycophyta (lycophytes)	seedless, vascular, leaves, roots, and stems	club mosses
Phylum Spenophyta	seedless, vascular, spore-producing	horsetails
Phylum Pterophyta	largest group of seedless, vascular plants	ferns
Phylum Cycadophyta	**gymnosperms**, vascular, naked seeds, simple cones, palm-shaped leaves	cycads
Phylum Gingkophyta	gymnosperms, seeds with fleshy outer layer	Ginkgo
Phylum Gnetophyta (gnetophytes)	gymnosperms	
Phylum Coniferophyta	most common gymnosperms, needle-like or scale-like leaves	
Family Pinaceae		pines, firs, spruces, hemlocks, larches, true cedars
Family Cupressaceae		junipers, cypresses
Family Taxodiaceae		redwoods, dawn redwood, bald cypress
Family Taxacea		yews
Phylum Anthophyta (**angiosperms**)	the flowering plants, largest group of vascular, seed-bearing plants; only organisms that have flowers and fruits	
Class Dicotyledonae **Dicotyledons** (**dicots**)	two **cotyledons**	
Family Nymphaceae		waterlilies
Family Papaveraceae		poppies
Family Brassicaceae		mustards, cabbages, radishes
Family Solanaceae		potatoes, aubergines, petunias
Family Salicaceae		willows, poplars
Family Rosaceae		roses, apples, almonds, strawberries
Family Fabaceae		peas, beans, lupins
Family Cactaceae		cacti
Family Cucurbitaceae		melons, cucumbers, squashes
Family Apiaceae		parsleys, carrots
Family Asteraceae		chrysanthemums, sunflowers, dandelions, lettuces
Class Monocotyledonae: **Monocotyledons** (**monocots**)	single cotyledon	
Family Liliaceae		lilies, hyacinths, tulips, onions, garlic
Family Iridaceae		irises, gladioli, crocuses
Family Orchidaceae		orchids
Family Arecaceae		date palms, coconut palms
Family Poaceae		grasses, bamboos, corn, wheat, sugarcane

Glossary

abscission zone area where part of a plant will separate from the main part of a plant

amyloplast structures found in the root cells of many plants; used for storing starch

angiosperm flowering plant

anther part of plant containing pollen

archaea (singular **archaean**) one of two types of prokaryote organisms, the other being the bacteria. Once included as part of the bacteria kingdom, the archaea are now considered by many scientists to form a kingdom of their own.

asexual reproduction reproduction in which offspring arise from a single parent and are genetically identical to, or clones of, that parent

bryophyte type of plant such as a moss or liverwort that has no xylem or phloem transportation system and requires the presence of free water to complete fertilization

carbohydrate chemical compound composed of carbon, hydrogen, and oxygen. Glucose is a simple carbohydrate.

carpel female reproductive organ in a flowering plant, made up of an ovary, a style, and a stigma, where pollen is received

cell membrane outer boundary of a cell, made of fat and protein molecules. It controls what enters and leaves the cell.

chlorophyll light-capturing pigment found in plant cells that is involved in photosynthesis; it gives plants their green color

chloroplasts organelles found in plant cells that contain chlorophyll; this is where photosynthesis takes place

chromoplasts structure in a plant cell that contains pigments; chloroplasts are a type of chromoplast containing the pigment chlorophyll

collenchyma simple plant tissue that provides support for primary growth

companion cells type of parenchyma specialized to help move materials into the sieve tube members that make up the conducting tubes in phloem

conifer type of gymnosperm, usually an evergreen tree or shrub with needle-like leaves

cotyledon seed leaf. Monocotyledon seeds have one cotyledon that stores enzymes for digesting the food stored in the seed. Dicotyledons have two cotyledons that store food for germination and early growth.

cuticle thin transparent covering of waxes and other materials on the outer cell walls of a plant's epidermis

cytoplasm all of the parts of a cell between the nucleus and the cell membrane

deciduous trees or shrubs that shed their leaves at the end of the growing season

dermal tissue tissues that cover and protect the outer surfaces of a plant

dicotyledon (often shortened to **dicot**) type of flowering plant that has two cotyledons (seed leaves) that provide a source of energy for the germinating seed

differentiate change from a simple structure to a more complex one

diffusion movement or mixing of substances as a result of the random motion of the molecules that make them up; movement tends to be from regions of high concentration to regions of low concentration

dormancy period during which the metabolic activity in an organism is greatly reduced; dormant seeds help a plant to survive unfavorable conditions

endosperm layer within a seed that acts as a food store for the plant embryo

enzymes class of proteins that act as biological catalysts. They greatly speed up the reactions that take place in cells.

epidermis outermost tissue layer of the plant

eukaryote cell that contains a nucleus and other organelles. All cells, with the exception of archaea and bacteria, are eukaryote cells.

fibrous root system branching network of roots growing from a young shoot; most monocots have fibrous root systems

gamete sex cell, such as an egg or sperm

gametophyte generation in the life cycle of a plant that produces the gametes

ground tissue tissue consisting of simple unspecialized cells that make up most of the bulk of a plant

guard cells two cells that lie next to each other in the surface of a plant's epidermis. When the cells swell with water an opening forms between them, called a stoma, through which carbon dioxide, oxygen, and water vapor can pass; when they lose water the stoma closes.

gymnosperm plant, such as a conifer, that has its seeds exposed rather than protected inside an ovary like they are in flowering plants

hyphae delicate filaments produced by fungi

lignin substance produced by plants to strengthen their tissues; it is the main constituent of wood

lipids oils, fats, waxes, and other fatty substances found in living cells

meristem regions of dividing cells in plants, such as shoot tips and root tips, where most growth takes place

mesophyll type of parenchyma where photosynthesis takes place. Palisade mesophyll cells are rodlike in shape and are attached to the upper epidermis of the leaf; they contain many chloroplasts. Spongy mesophyll, below the palisade mesophyll, is less regular in shape and contains fewer chloroplasts.

metabolism total of the chemical reactions in a cell by which it acquires and uses energy for all activities that go on inside it

Glossary

minerals simple chemical substances required by organisms to function healthily; plants get minerals from the soil, animals get minerals in their food

molecules particles made up of two or more atoms joined together

monocotyledon (often shortened to **monocot**) type of flowering plant that has a single cotyledon, or seed leaf, which provides a source of energy for the germinating seed

mutualism type of symbiosis in which both species benefit from the relationship

mycelium network of hyphae that form a fungus

mycorrhiza form of mutualism between the hyphae of a fungus and the roots of a plant

nucleus (plural **nuclei**) large organelle in the center of a cell where its genetic material is held

organelle one of several different structures, surrounded by a membrane, found in eukaryote cells. The cell nucleus and plant chloroplasts are two types of organelle.

osmosis diffusion of water between two regions of different concentration separated by a partially permeable membrane

ovary enlarged base of one or more carpels in a flowering plant

ovule part of a plant ovary that develops into a seed when fertilized

parenchyma simple tissue made up of loosely packed thin-walled cells that makes up the bulk of a plant

petals often colorful parts of a flower the function of which is to attract pollinators such as insects

petiole stalk that joins the leaf to the stem

phloem tissue forming part of a plant's vascular system that carries sugars and other dissolved substances through the plant; made up of living sieve cells connected to form tubes and companion cells that help move substances into the tubes

photosynthesis process by which green plants and some other organisms use the energy of sunlight to assemble glucose from carbon dioxide and water

plumule part of a seed that will develop into the plant shoot and carry the first true leaves

pollen tiny grains that carry the male sex cells of flowering plants

pollination process by which pollen is transferred from the male reproductive organs of a flower to the female reproductive organs of the same or a different flower

primary growth lengthening of shoots and roots as a plant grows

prokaryote cell that does not have its genetic material enclosed in a nucleus. All archaea and bacteria are prokaryotes.

protein one of a group of complex organic molecules that perform a variety of essential tasks in cells, including providing structure and acting as catalysts (enzymes) in chemical reactions

radicle first root to grow from a seed when it germinates

respiration process by which living things obtain oxygen from the environment to be used in the breakdown and release of energy from their food

root system parts of a plant below ground that take up water and help anchor the plant

sclerenchyma simple plant tissue with thick-walled cells that supports mature plant parts and protects seeds

secondary growth thickening of older stems and roots as a plant grows

sepal part of a plant formed from modified leaves that surrounds and protects a flower bud

sexual reproduction reproduction involving the formation of male and female sex cells, or gametes, and their joining together in the process of fertilization; the offspring inherit characteristics from both male and female parents and are unique individuals

shoot system parts of a plant that are above ground, such as the leaves, stem, and flowers

sieve plate perforated cell wall that allows liquid to flow between sieve tube members

sieve tube members cells that join together to form the tubes that make up phloem

stamen male reproductive organ of a flowering plant, often consisting of a long stalk with an anther at the tip where pollen is formed

stigma sticky or hairy part of a carpel that captures pollen grains

stomata (singular **stoma**) gaps or openings between guard cells on the surface of a plant's epidermis that open and close to control the movement into the plant of carbon dioxide and the movement out of oxygen and water vapor

style core of the stem

succulents plants with thick, fleshy, water-storing tissues, adapted to live where water is scarce

symbiosis relationship in which individuals of one species live alongside, in, or on, members of another species for at least part of their life cycle

taproot system root system with a single main root, or tap root, from which other roots branch off; most dicots have taproot systems

tissue group of cells of the same type that work together to perform a particular task in a multi-cellular organism

tracheids one of the cell types, along with vessel members, that form xylem

transpiration loss of water from the above ground parts of a plant, especially from the leaves

vacuole fluid-filled cavity inside a cell that is surrounded by a membrane

vascular system system for transporting water and other material through a vascular plant

vascular tissue tissues, xylem, and phloem, forming a vascular system through which water and other materials are transported through a vascular plant

vegetative reproduction form of asexual reproduction where new plants develop from multi-cellular structures that become detached from the parent plant

vessel members one of the cell types, along with tracheids, that form xylem; their walls form part of the xylem pipelines

xylem tissue forming part of a plant's vascular system. Xylem cells form pipelines of interconnecting cells that carry water and dissolved substances through the plant. Xylem cells die when they reach maturity.

Further Reading and Websites

Books

Morgan, Sally. *Green Plants.* Chicago: Heinemann Library, 2006.

Spillsbury, Richard and Louise. *Plant Classification: The Life of Plants.* Chicago: Heinemann Library, 2002.

Wallace, Holly. *Life Processes: Cells and Systems.* Chicago: Heinemann Library, 2007.

Websites

Flowering Plant Diversity (http://scitec.uwichill.edu.bb/bcs/bl14apl/flow2.htm)
> An introduction to the diversity of flowering plants.

Flowering Plants (http://waynesword.palomar.edu/trmar98.htm)
> A colorful introduction to the world of flowering plants.

Plantlife International (www.plantlife.org.uk)
> Plantlife International works for the conservation of wild plants throughout the world.

What Is Photosynthesis? (http://photoscience.la.asu.edu/photosyn/education/learn.html#amazing)
> An Arizona State University site with links to many articles on photosynthesis.

Index